Phases of Love

Dr Diksha Sirohi

BookLeaf
Publishing

Presentation by *BookLeaf Publishing*

Web: www.bookleafpub.com

E-mail: info@bookleafpub.com

ISBN: 9789357612715

First edition 2022

DEDICATION

To all the hearts that experience the phases of love.

ACKNOWLEDGEMENT

To my family and friends who have stood by me in myriad ways, I am thankful for your love and patience.

PREFACE

This story is about Lisha. Like others of her age,
Lisha (21) too falls in the ocean named Love.
Navigating the stormy and adventurous realms
of this ocean, Lisha discovers its many phases.

The book begins with poetry on finding love and
in the end finding yourself. It ends with
discovering a spiritual bond between soulmates
and knowing that love finally remains a lasting
universal force through all its phases. The poems
presented here can be read in any order. But if
you would like to delve deeper to find a magical
flow, reading from start to end is recommended.

You are invited to dive into Lisha's ocean and
swim with her into the poetic phases of love.

Her Eyes

There's something in those deep brown eyes,
That silently speak to my weary soul.
Merging my loose ends into meaningful ties,
They mend my life and make me whole.

A thousand attempts, I lose in vain,
The chemistry of love is unknown.
All I can say is, she holds my rein,
When she glances and I am softly blown.

Eyes that change with every touch,
Tightly shut in a hungry moan,
Or pinning looks when she longs me much,
Or beaming eyes when I am her very own.

Love's Elixir

Pour me that love,
From those drunk eyes,
I will soak the amorous vibes,
Taking you away from the world's true lies.

Sing me that love song,
From your beautiful lips,
Like it were the only melody,
On a full moon's eclipse.

Bring to my senses,
The pleasure of your touch,
Drenching my pores and skin.
In liquid love, I would want very much.

Give me your time, your life and love,
Through days of summer and winter,
I'd turn it into a warm home,
The recipe of Love's Elixir.

Dusk

3

Play your fingers on my lips,
Let there be showers of rain,
Let there be the melody of a song,
To drown a stabbingly lonely pain.

The Sun is setting in an orange hue,
Casting long naked shadows on the wall,
Wrapped into each other's amorous aura,
Sprayed with lust, in love we fall.

Finding Herself

These lines I cross with you,

<pre>
Are lines I   C   S
                        \   /
                          R
                        /   \
                       S   O
</pre>

<pre>
To enter my   S----->O
                       | |
                       L<------U
</pre>

Few Minutes

I loved the few minutes you were here,
Helping me hold on to life and breath near.
On cold nights, your warm hands held mine,
Soothing my soul, forging a connection divine.

I know for sure, in this frantic need to survive,
We've come a long way, treading many a lives,
My soul has known yours for an eternal time,
This ain't a passing breeze, but love of all-time.

Few minutes I say, are but a life-time,
In the cosmic play of the universal chime,
We tread the space once again through stardust,
Traversing galaxies, healing with soul trust.

Cloud and Sea

Love like the cloud and sea
They have a unique chemistry.

One evaporates to fill the other,
and the other empties to fill the one.

The Broken Heart

It ached and pained, the heart bled red,
To know you were gone that far ahead.
I gave you my soul, my love and flesh,
My trust and care and everything else.

I love you much, though you broke my heart,
Not to mention of my soul being torn apart.
Your love was the poison, I chose to drink,
While you walked away, I chose to sink.

I sulked for long, till I could think no more,
Of how you walked away with a dame, so cold.
The plunge seemed easy, on that dreary night,
Than the thought of living without you in sight.

I took one step, and then another,
With no one to stop me and none to bother.
I jumped that cliff, drowning into the sea,
From where your ship, sailed away in glee.

My love for you alas, didn't die with me,
My soul lingers on, like a flower's bee.
I'd wish you'd come and see me on that shore,
I still love you much, from the deepest core.

Lost

They wrote essays on loving someone,
And elaborate descriptions on intimacy,
Then came along the romantic gestures in heaps
and tons,
Followed by quotes on honesty and integrity.

But no one thought to mourn the loss of love,
In the hollow autumn that blows away the leaf,
Where does the pain go, as the soul is stripped?
The lonely branch bearing a chilly grief?

Shielded in the warm embrace of earth,
Rejoicing the winter with a new companion,
While I shiver bare in the white snow dust,
Overlooking a cold, deep, dark canyon.

No one taught to mourn this loss.
That wrenches the soul in tightening knots.
No one taught to mourn this loss,
Perhaps a respite - a wooden cross?

The Last Breath?

The midnight oil burned besides me.
I lay there wondering,
If this was going to be my last breath,
Wondering if this was the last flicker of the
lamp,
If this was the last of the starlight I was to see.

Until, he called to say,
he would see me another day.

That moment, I decided to live.
Only this time, for myself.

Unspoken Words

The tongue that speaks a thousand tales,
Of mountain, seas and sturdy sails.

But not the tales that the eyes narrate,
Those unspoken words, that empty slate.

Letting Go

It was possible for me
to love him.

And therefore I,
LET GO.

Scars

The pain that remained,
When you left,
Developed into scars on my skin.
But that is a good thing.

Because scars teach us,
that wounds heal.
And we become better people,
Capable of loving again.

Ocean's Daughter

Jump oh darling, if you must,
Over those cliffs into the ocean,
Sprinkle your dreams, be a wanderlust,
Fuel the adventure and emotion.

Deep in those unchartered waters,
In the azure of the blankness,
There dwell a billion creatures,
Flowing in the zeal of liveliness.

Leave the staleness on the hard soil,
Swim with mermaids deep into the caves,
Freshen your soul with the water's oil,
With a surf or two, riding under the waves.

When you return to the shore on the land,
The ocean would have blessed your soul,
Ocean's daughter you'd be, not that of the sand,
For dreams now would be lived and told.

Dandelion

Have you ever watched a dandelion?
What did it teach you?

Me?

It taught me that,
Letting go is a beautiful process.

Watch the delicate strands float away,
Light into the wind,
Heave your heart into the air,
Let the wind carry away your cares.

Watch them float away,
Let it GO.
It isn't as hard as it SEEMS.

The Frozen Lake

15

You turned cold like a frozen lake.
I didn't know which part of you I could tap into.
You would either swallow me up or refuse to
open at all.
When I started loving the warm Sun,
You began to melt furiously.

But Love my dear, doesn't come in seasons.

Soulmate

Winds blow across the Southern side,
Among the crowd, there is a face that hides,
I can tell the face is the other half,
Oh! an ache in my heart the wind
choreographed.

An ache that feels as sweet as love,
Sugar to my spice, an olive to my dove,
Mate to my soul, an anchor to my boat,
Yin to my yang, an end to my quote.

Twilight Halo

17

Dark clouds gathered and thunder roared,
Amidst strangers, my heart beat soared,
Brilliant white flashes struck the earth,
An impatient wait was sprinkled with mirth.

He walked across the hall, too handsome to
miss,
Wet in the rain, the lightening saw us kiss,
My heart skipped a beat, cheeks pink blushed,
The street lamp witnessed our passions rushed.

Cupid struck the arrow, my heart swells in love,
Our souls sync together and I am in awe,
Walks by the beach in the sunset yellow,
A love is born in the twilight halo.

Winter Love

18

Watching the drifting mist float by,
On a cold winter morning,
Reminiscing the warmth of his hugs,
She dropped him a quote of love,
Stronger and warmer than
His morning coffee!

Breathing Love

19

He looked at her,
And closed his eyes,
Taking in a long deep breath,
As if, breathing her love,
Like she was a freshly blossomed rose.

Gratitude

To the relationships that turned sour,
I do not despise you.
Your presence (and then absence),
Taught me the strength of letting go.

To the friendships that turned sour,
I do not despise you.
Your presence (and then absence),
Taught me tolerance and patience.

To all the relationships that turned sour,
I do not despise you.
Rather
I thank you all, for the good times we shared,
For the coffee dates,
For the smiles and tears.

And

Above all, I thank you all
For the LOVE we had,
No matter how momentary.

Love is All

21

Love isn't a state to FALL in.

Love is a state to BE in.